The ABC's of Philadelphia

An Illustrated Guide to the City of Brotherly Love

Written by Greg Landry
Designed and Illustrated by Robert Hochgertel

Camino Books, Inc.
Philadelphia

Manufactured in the United States of America

1 2 3 4 5 14 13 12

Library of Congress Cataloging-in-Publication Data

Landry, Greg, 1968-.
ABC's of Philadelphia: an illustrated guide to the city of brotherly love / written by Greg Landry; designed and illustrated by Robert Hochgertel.
p. cm.
ISBN 978-1-933822-05-1 (alk. paper)
1. Philadelphia (Pa.)—Pictorial works. 2. Philadelphia (Pa.)—Description and travel. 3. Philadelphia (Pa.)—In art. I. Hochgertel, Robert, 1962-. II. Title.

F158.37.L36 2009
974.8'11—dc22   2008047267

Cover (depicting City Hall), interior design, and illustrations: Robert Hochgertel

Notes on artwork depicted in this book:

C - Signers' Hall sculptures designed by StudioEIS with historical consultation by Raymond Smock
F - *Benjamin Franklin National Memorial,* sculpture by James Earle Fraser
K - *John B. Kelly (The Rower),* sculpture by Harry Rosin
N - *Tamanend,* sculpture by Raymond Sandoval
R - *Lion Crushing a Serpent,* sculpture by Antoine-Louis Barye
S - *Swann Memorial Fountain (or The Fountain of Three Rivers)* by Alexander Stirling Calder, sculptor; Wilson Eyre, Jr., architect
   William Penn, sculpture by Alexander Milne Calder

This book is available at a special discount on bulk purchases for promotional, business, and educational use.

Publisher
Camino Books, Inc.
P.O. Box 59026
Philadelphia, PA 19102
www.caminobooks.com

Dedicated to Katherine and Thomas, that they may enjoy all Philadelphia has to offer.
—G.L.

Dedicated to my daughters Alexis and Ainsley.
Thank you for inspiring me to see the beauty of this city all over again through your eyes.
—R.H.

The author and artist wish to thank Barbara Gibbons for helping to shepherd this book through completion.

"A great city is that which has the greatest men and women...."

—Walt Whitman
From "Song of the Broad-Axe," first published in 1856, in *Leaves of Grass*

Walt Whitman, one of America's greatest poets, lived approximately the last 20 years of his life in neighboring Camden, New Jersey, across the Delaware River from Philadelphia. Upon his death in 1892, thousands paid tribute to him. A bridge connecting Pennsylvania and New Jersey, completed in 1957, is named in his honor.

A CITY OF ART
Museums and sculptures, gardens and fountains, murals everywhere you look

Philadelphia is among the world's great art destinations. Within just a few city blocks along the picturesque Ben Franklin Parkway there are many prominent museums including the grand Philadelphia Museum of Art, the Rodin Museum and the new city campus of the legendary Barnes Foundation. Collectively here you will find over 180 Renoirs, 70 Cézannes and the most extensive collection of Auguste Rodin's work outside of France. The city is also home to more outdoor art than any other American City.

Boathouse row

In bright outline at night, shining along the Schuylkill

Various rowing clubs own buildings along the Schuylkill River, forming an often-photographed cluster called Boathouse Row. During the day, the architectural detail and variety of color are prominent. At night, the perspective changes, with each clubhouse's shape outlined in bright lights 365 days a year.

C OUR CONSTITUTION

The resilient framework of our government, a living document, amended over time

James Madison was considered the "Father of the Constitution." During the summer of 1787, he led the efforts of the Constitutional Convention to draft the supreme law of the nation. Their achievement is celebrated in Signers' Hall at the National Constitution Center.

D DECLARATION OF INDEPENDENCE
"Life, Liberty and the pursuit of Happiness"

The Second Continental Congress formally accepted the Declaration on July 4, 1776, at Independence Hall. Built between 1732 and 1753, Independence Hall served as the State House of the Province of Pennsylvania. It is often referred to as the birthplace of the nation because of the number and importance of historic events that took place there.

EASTERN STATE PENITENTIARY
"Confinement in solitude with labor"

Eastern State Penitentiary, opened in 1829, was designed with a new philosophy of criminal treatment in mind—to create a penitent individual through enforced isolation. Decades of construction and changes in criminal justice policy led to the structure now in place. It ceased operation as a prison in 1971. Tours and events are currently scheduled throughout the year.

THE **F**RANKLIN INSTITUTE
The science museum honoring Philadelphia's greatest citizen

Benjamin Franklin—scientist, inventor, diplomat, politician, and man of commerce—was renowned for his book, Experiments and Observations in Electricity. One of his many significant accomplishments, it was considered among the most important works of science in the world upon publication in 1751.

HISTORIC BARTRAM'S GARDEN

America's oldest living botanical garden

The home of John Bartram, America's first botanist, is a National Historic Landmark situated on 45 acres of meadow, wetland, and parkland. Dozens of other public gardens and arboreta dot the Delaware Valley; some of the more well known include Chanticleer Garden, Morris Arboretum, Longwood Gardens, and Winterthur.

H CITY HALL
Where gargoyles perch

A stunning structure built in the late 19th century, City Hall is located at the intersection of Market and Broad streets and is the center of municipal government. It is capped with a statue of William Penn, and as the result of a "gentlemen's agreement" among planners and developers, no building in Center City surpassed its height until 1987.

ITALIAN MARKET

The tastes and aromas of fresh pastas and cheeses, breads and meats, fruits and sweets

For 100 years, purveyors of Italian fare have gathered on 9th Street, offering a wide assortment of ingredients to gourmets and family cooks. The market has become more international, as Chinese, Korean, and Mexican vendors have added to the variety.

J
JEWELERS' ROW
The nation's oldest diamond district, a rich history indeed

Dating from 1851, Jewelers' Row is the second largest such district in the country. More than 300 jewelers and craftsmen offer precious gems of every shape, size, and price, all within the area bounded by 7th, 8th, Chestnut, and Walnut streets.

KELLY DRIVE
Winding through Fairmount Park

Kelly Drive takes its name from John B. Kelly, Sr., former President of the Fairmount Park Commission, accomplished rower, and father of actress Grace Kelly. Its setting along the Schuylkill River is ideal for cycling, running, walking, rollerblading, and even rock climbing.

LIBERTY BELL
Our beloved national symbol

Cast in 1752, the Liberty Bell first became an icon for liberty when it was adopted as a symbol for the abolitionist movement in 1837. In the 1880s, the Bell's prominence increased as it was exhibited at many fairs and expositions throughout the country.

MEMORIAL HALL

Commemorating soldiers of the American Revolution

Designed for the 1876 Centennial Exposition, Memorial Hall is another grand attraction of Fairmount Park, Philadelphia's park system. At the turn of the 20th century, it displayed the city's art collection before the Philadelphia Museum of Art opened. It is now home to the Please Touch Museum—the children's museum of Philadelphia.

NATIVE AMERICANS
The Lenni Lenape, original inhabitants of the Delaware Valley

The Lenni Lenape—at one time led by the revered Chief Tamanend, commemorated in a sculpture at Penn's Landing—broke apart under pressure from European immigrant expansion, with different factions moving over many years. One of the largest groups of descendants eventually settled in what is now Oklahoma.

THE PHILADELPHIA **O**RCHESTRA
Acclaimed throughout the world

Maestros of distinction, such as Leopold Stokowski and Eugene Ormandy, have led The Philadelphia Orchestra. One of America's "Big Five" symphony orchestras, it performs from September to May at the Kimmel Center for the Performing Arts, located at the corner of Broad and Spruce streets.

PENN'S LANDING

Where William Penn first set foot in Philadelphia

William Penn first arrived in 1682 after King Charles II chartered Pennsylvania to him in exchange for cancelling a debt owed to William's father. Penn's Landing encompasses the place where he is reported to have first stepped into his "greene countrie towne." These days, Penn's Landing is the venue for a variety of cultural events, concerts, and activities scheduled throughout the year, including annual July 4th fireworks.

QUAKER TRADITIONS
Friendship, meditation, and toleration

William Penn's Quaker views on religious tolerance were precursors of the ideals of our nation. He wrote, "If any person shall abuse or deride any other for his, or her, different persuasion and practice in matters of religion, such a person shall be looked upon as a Disturber of the peace...." Meetings among the Friends are regularly held at the Arch Street Meeting House, built in 1804.

RITTENHOUSE SQUARE
Part of Philadelphia's original design

In 1682, William Penn and surveyor Thomas Holmes designed Philadelphia as a grid, considered innovative at the time. Center Square (where City Hall is now located) was situated at the heart of the plan with four additional parks spaced throughout the original quadrants, defined by the major north-south (now Broad) and east-west (now Market) streets. The southwest park was named Rittenhouse Square in 1825.

SWANN MEMORIAL FOUNTAIN
The oasis in Logan Square

Located in another of William Penn's five original squares, Swann Memorial Fountain faces the Philadelphia Museum of Art at the midpoint of the Ben Franklin Parkway. The fountain's designer, Alexander Stirling Calder, was son of the Calder who sculpted City Hall's William Penn and father of the Calder who created the art museum's famed mobiles. Native American figures sit at the fountain's center, symbolizing the Schuylkill, the Delaware, and the Wissahickon, the area's three chief waterways.

THE WILMA THEATER

Bold design, and performance, on the Avenue of the Arts

Many wonderful theaters about town and along the Avenue of the Arts (the aptly named corridor of Broad Street—north of City Hall to Lehigh, south to Washington, east to 13th, and west to 18th) present entertainment for all audiences, from Broadway-style musicals to children's theater and puppetry. The Theatre Alliance of Greater Philadelphia, composed of over 100 theaters and affiliated organizations, annually holds The Barrymore Awards for Excellence in Theatre, named after the family of actors originally from Philadelphia.

UNIVERSITY OF PENNSYLVANIA
A member of the Ivy League and the Philadelphia Big 5

The University of Pennsylvania is one of the region's 80 or so colleges and universities, which are attended by a total of approximately 300,000 students. Besides the Big 5—comprising La Salle, St. Joseph's, Temple, and Villanova universities, in addition to Penn—other notables include Arcadia and Drexel universities, and Bryn Mawr, Chestnut Hill, Haverford, and Swarthmore colleges.

THE ROAR OF VICTORY

For Philly's beloved teams and famous athletes

Adjacent modern sports venues in South Philly are home to the city's professional franchises—the Eagles, Phillies, Flyers, and 76ers. A legendary boxing heritage and nationally known events such as the Penn Relays—one of the largest U.S. track and field meets—professional championship cycling, and rowing regattas generate additional excitement. Year-round, passions run high for Philadelphia's famously loyal and knowledgeable fans.

FAIRMOUNT **W**ATER WORKS
Greek temples on the Schuylkill

Renowned for its beauty and technological achievement (at the time of construction, said to be the longest dam in the world), the Fairmount Water Works was one of the most popular tourist attractions in the United States. During much of the 19th century, it was second only to Niagara Falls.

eXTRAORDINARY NEIGHBORHOODS
The pulse of Philadelphia

Each neighborhood in this city of neighborhoods maintains a strong, distinctive identity, contributing to the trendy and traditional mix that is Philadelphia. Cherished for their culture and quirks, their food and ethnic heritage, some of the more popular are Chinatown—famous for its Friendship Arch at 10th and Arch streets—Manayunk, Chestnut Hill, and Society Hill.

Y

Yo!
Meet me on South Street

An expression of greeting or a way to get attention, the word yo gained popularity in the streets of Philadelphia. Yo conjures images of movie hero Rocky Balboa ("Yo, Adrian!") running up the art museum steps, life in the neighborhoods, and Philly traditions like eating cheesesteaks or soft pretzels on South Street—a famous youth culture destination filled with tattoo parlors and eclectic shops and restaurants.

PHILADELPHIA ZOO

Home to antelope, bears, crocodiles...and zebras

Though last in the alphabet, the Zoo was yet another Philadelphia first (along with first hospital, library, university, fire company, and computer, to mention just a few). It opened its doors on July 1, 1874, under the direction of the Zoological Society of Philadelphia, which was established in 1859.

WHERE TO FIND IT
Philadelphia — Block by Block

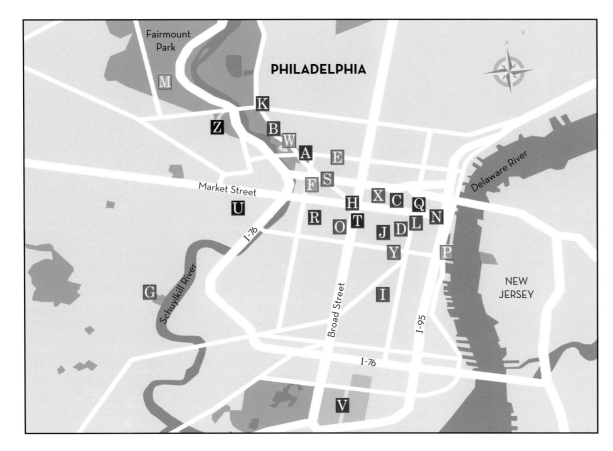

L LIBERTY BELL
Liberty Bell Center
Market Street between 5th & 6th streets

M MEMORIAL HALL
4231 North Concourse Drive

N NATIVE AMERICANS
Statue of Chief Tamanend
Front & Market streets

O THE PHILADELPHIA ORCHESTRA
Kimmel Center for the Performing Arts
300 South Broad Street

P PENN'S LANDING
Between Market & South streets on the
waterfront along the Delaware River

Q QUAKER TRADITIONS
Arch Street Meeting House
320 Arch Street

R RITTENHOUSE SQUARE
18th & Walnut streets

S SWANN MEMORIAL FOUNTAIN
Logan Circle on the Benjamin Franklin Parkway

T THE WILMA THEATER
265 South Broad Street

U UNIVERSITY OF PENNSYLVANIA
Furness Library
220 South 34th Street

V THE ROAR OF VICTORY
South Philadelphia Sports Complex
South end of Broad Street at Pattison Avenue

W FAIRMOUNT WATER WORKS
640 Waterworks Drive

X EXTRAORDINARY NEIGHBORHOODS
Friendship Arch
10th & Arch streets

Y YO! MEET ME ON SOUTH STREET
The stretch of South Street between
Front & 10th streets

Z PHILADELPHIA ZOO
3400 West Girard Avenue

A A CITY OF ART
Philadelphia Museum of Art
26th Street & the Benjamin Franklin Parkway

B BOATHOUSE ROW
Kelly Drive, East Fairmount Park

C OUR CONSTITUTION
National Constitution Center
525 Arch Street

D DECLARATION OF INDEPENDENCE
Independence Hall
313 Walnut Street

E EASTERN STATE PENITENTIARY
2124 Fairmount Avenue

F THE FRANKLIN INSTITUTE
222 North 20th Street

G HISTORIC BARTRAM'S GARDEN
54th Street & Lindbergh Boulevard

H CITY HALL
Broad & Market streets

I ITALIAN MARKET
South 9th Street

J JEWELERS' ROW
Sansom Street between 7th & 8th streets

K KELLY DRIVE
Four winding miles along the Schuylkill River